KU-197-768

Be Happy

Be Happy

170 ways to transform your day

Patrick Lindsay

hardie grant books
MELBOURNE · LONDON

Published in 2010
Hardie Grant Books
85 High Street
Prahran, Victoria 3181, Australia
www.hardiegrant.com.au

Cataloguing-in-Publication data is available from the National
Library of Australia.
Be Happy: 170 ways to transform your day
ISBN 978 1 74066 963 4

Jacket design and illustration by Luisa Laino Design & Illustration
Typeset in 10/12pt The Sans Light by Cannon Typesetting
Printed and bound in China by C & C Offset Printing Co.

10 9 8 7 6 5 4 3 2 1

Be happy ...

Follow your heart

First, know your heart.
It knows things your mind can't understand.
Listen to it.
Listen above the crowd.
Be open to it.
Let it guide you on the big decisions.
Be true to it.

The heart has its reasons, which reason knows nothing of.

Blaise Pascal

Be happy ...

Be faithful

It sounds so old-fashioned.
But fidelity is the foundation of so many valuable things,
like love,
mateship
and family.
Most importantly, be faithful to yourself.
And your core beliefs.

Live your beliefs and you can turn the world around.

Henry David Thoreau

Be happy ...

Accentuate the positive

Too often we dwell on the negatives.
This weighs us down.
Look for the upside.
See light rather than the dark side.
Search for positive energy.
It will transform your attitude.
It will empower you
and reignite your passion.

Keep sowing your seeds, for you never know which one will grow—
perhaps they all will.

The Bible

Be happy ...

Explore a mystery

Take the challenge.
Back your judgement.
Draw on your experience.
Look with different eyes.
Ask questions,
especially the obvious ones.
Go back to the original sources.
Crosscheck them.
Begin to unravel it.

Be an opener of doors.

Ralph Waldo Emerson

Be happy ...

Stop complaining

Grizzling achieves nothing.
Just stirs animosity,
promotes negatives
and excuses.
Look through others' eyes.
Seek solutions.
Make positive suggestions.
Help implement them.
You'll be surprised at your reception.

Never complain, never explain.

Benjamin Disraeli

Be happy ...

Take the path least travelled

It takes courage and confidence.
It has some risks but it often brings great rewards:
the challenge of the new,
the thrill of exploration,
growth from learning
and self-confidence from success.

We know what happens to people who stay in the middle of the road.
They get run over.

Aneurin Bevan

Be happy ...

Remember people's names

It seems such a small thing to you.
But it's so important to others.
And so memorable.
When you're introduced, greet people by name.
Make a mental note.
Associate the name with the face.
If you take the trouble to remember someone's name,
they'll remember you
and hold you in high regard.

A man dies and leaves a name; a tiger dies and leaves a skin.
Chinese saying

Be happy ...

Be patient

With experience we realise the importance of patience.
Too many decisions are reflex actions.
Take the time to ponder.
Put things in perspective.
Allow situations to develop.
Sense the patterns of things.
Wait until the moment is right.
Then be decisive.

Can you remain unmoving until the right action arises by itself?
Tao Te Ching

Be happy ...

Be honest with yourself

We can fool others.
But we can't fool ourselves.
Being honest with yourself brings freedom.
Work towards self-acceptance.
Respect yourself as you would want
others to respect you.
Find your truths.
Aspire to be a better person.

An honest man is the noblest work of God.

Alexander Pope

Be happy ...

Enjoy the trip

No matter how far you travel
or how long the trip—
across the city,
across the country,
across the world,
or through your life—
the journey matters more than the destination.
Enjoy the journey.

Each journey starts with the first step.

Chinese proverb

Be happy ...

Do your best

How often we say it.
How often we promise to do it.
Yet how rarely do we actually do the best we can.
When we do—
when we use all our efforts,
when we push through old boundaries—
the satisfaction is enormous.
And the rewards are sweeter because
they've been earned.

Make the most of yourself, for that is all there is of you.
Ralph Waldo Emerson

Be happy ...

Return your calls

It's so easy to ignore messages.
Sometimes it's justified.
Put yourself in the caller's shoes.
There's nothing worse than being ignored.
You're bigger than that.
Give a little of yourself.
Give others the courtesy you'd hope to receive.
Whether they're phone calls or calls for help,
answer them.
In the long-term you'll be the winner.

There are only the pursued, the pursuing, the busy and the tired.
F. Scott Fitzgerald

Be happy ...

Help the earth

We're only borrowing the earth while we're here.
We must hand it on to the next generation.
Let's do what we can to improve it.
Or at least do as little damage as possible.
Do the simple things.
Recycle.
Join in community clean-ups.
Try solar energy.
Walk, cycle, car-pool, catch a bus.
Watch over our oceans.
Protect the forests.

The world is a fine place and worth fighting for.

Ernest Hemingway

Be happy ...

Free-fall

Most of our lives are structured.
Most of our actions planned.
Most of our risks covered.
All the more reason to free-fall sometimes.
Go with your instincts.
Let your heart lead.
Take a chance.

Freedom has a thousand charms to show.
That slaves, howe'er contented, never know.

William Cowper

Be happy ...

Set goals

They give direction and purpose
and a sense of optimism.
But paint with a broad brush.
Fill in the details as needed.
Plan for tomorrow
but live a day at a time.

We never prepared one battle plan without at least one alternate plan.
General George S. Patton

Be happy ...

Listen to the rain

Let it soothe your spirit.
Smell the freshness.
Hear the patterns.
See the cleansing.
The way trees and plants drink it in.
Feel the renewal.

The sound of the rain is like the voices of tens of thousands of monks reading sutras.

Yukio Mishima

Be happy ...

Walk through the bush

Feel the power in your legs.
The strength in your lungs.
Soak up the sounds of the birds
and the wind.
Enjoy the scents
and the colours of the season.
Observe the cycles of birth and growth,
death and regrowth.

Your house shall not be an anchor but a mast.

Kahlil Gibran

Be happy ...

Skinny-dip in the sea

Be bold.
Let the ocean carry you
and caress you.
Feel its endless rhythm
and power.
Let the salt water heal you.
Explore its depths.
Adopt its freedom.

I have bathed in the Poem of the Sea.

Arthur Rimbaud

Be happy ...

Walk barefoot

Feel the sand between your toes
and the living grass.
The warmth of the sun on the road.
Connect with the earth.
Feel its textures.
Enliven your senses.
Savour the freedom.

Adopt the pace of nature: her secret is patience.

Ralph Waldo Emerson

Be happy ...

Change direction

Even a small change can reap big benefits.
Consider alternatives.
Look with fresh eyes.
Register patterns.
Feel where you are blocked or stale.
Try something new.
Start with small things and experience the difference.
Then you'll see the more important changes
and you'll make them naturally.

True life is lived when tiny changes occur.

Leo Tolstoy

Be happy ...

Pause awhile

We all need time to reflect,
to put things in perspective,
to truly value things in our lives
and to appreciate them.
To reflect properly,
we must be calm and balanced.
Put your life on pause.
Sit on a quiet beach
or in a tranquil garden.
Somewhere you can muse without distraction.
Calmness and balance will join you there.

The hardest thing to see is what is in front of your eyes.
Johann Wolfgang von Goethe

Be happy ...

Look at the big picture

Too often, life pushes in on us.
It narrows our vision.
Listen without filtering.
Observe without prejudice.
Allow things to wash over you and open your mind.
See things against the past.
Consider them in the light of the future.
Take an expansive view.

What lies behind us and what lies before us are tiny matters compared to what lies within us.

Ralph Waldo Emerson

Be happy ...

Enjoy the silence

In a world of constant clamour,
silence can be pure pleasure.
It can provide a haven
and allow your own melodies to flourish.
Seek out the quiet corners.
Enjoy the liberating space they provide.
Fill the silent space with calm thoughts
and revive your spirits.

Silence is golden.

Proverb

Be happy ...

Make a comeback

Whatever the position,
whatever the expectations,
you're always in the game
if you believe you're in the game.
You have the power.
With self-belief and determination, you can change
your fortunes.
You can turn things around.
You can come back.

Never give in. Never give in. Never give in.

Winston Churchill

Be happy ...

Ignore the pessimists

Avoid their company
and their dark vibes.
They thrive on failure and negativity.
Rise above them.
Trust your instincts and your ability.
Set your own standards and goals.
Aim high.
Strive for great things.

The optimist proclaims that we live in the best of all possible worlds;
the pessimist fears this is true.

James Branch Cabell

Be happy ...

Stop being a victim

Take a hard look at yourself.
Are you a willing victim?
Do you take the line of least resistance
then blame others,
or circumstances,
or fate?
It's a matter of pride and self-respect,
and the respect of others.
Stand up for yourself, for your rights, for your beliefs.
Others will appreciate your efforts.
And, surprisingly, many will help you.

Life is either a daring adventure or nothing.

Helen Keller

Be happy ...

Stop underestimating yourself

Too often we take ourselves for granted,
or worse, we only see our failures,
mistakes or imperfections.
Give yourself credit where it's due.
Look at the other side of the ledger.
Start appreciating your achievements.
Understand how you reached them.
Recall the satisfaction of a job well done.
Build on that feeling.
Seek to duplicate it.

Never desert your own line of talent.

Sydney Smith

Be happy ...

Take a cryptic challenge

It's mental Mount Everest to most of us,
but it's all in our mindset.
Warm up with quick or simple puzzles.
Use a dictionary or thesaurus when you're stuck.
Take your time and gain confidence.
Step up to the cryptic challenge.
Look through the writer's eyes.
Learn the language of the game.
Persist until you see patterns.
Then it will open for you.

With words we govern men.

Benjamin Disraeli

Be happy ...

Visit a friend

A surprise visit is a great gift to a friend.
It shows you've been thinking of them.
It shows how much you value their friendship.
It will lift their spirits.
It will warm up your day.

We can do no great things—only small things with great love.
Katherine Mansfield

Be happy ...

Go back to your roots

Rewind your life.
Spool through the memories.
Relive some of the highlights.
Recall some of the characters who travelled with you.
Revisit some of the places that helped form your views.
See how far you've travelled.
Discover the things that matter.
Cherish them.

To understand where you are going you must understand
where you come from.

Celtic proverb

Be happy ...

Look in the mirror

Take a long look.
Peer deeply into your eyes.
Try to see behind the façade.
What kind of person are you?
Do you like what you see?
Do the good things outweigh the bad?
Work on yourself so that they do.

In youth we learn; in age we understand.

Marie Ebner-Eschenbach

Be happy ...

Reward yourself

It's a question of balance.
Don't take it too far and become selfish,
but don't ignore yourself.
Be honest.
When you deserve it, reward yourself.
We all respond to positive reinforcement.

Self is a sea boundless and measureless.

Kahlil Gibran

Be happy ...

Visualise your dream

Picture yourself achieving your goals.
Place yourself in the picture.
Think deeply on it
and you'll be surprised how often your visualisation
becomes reality.

Live the life you've imagined.

Henry David Thoreau

Be happy ...

Be ready

Opportunity often knocks on empty doors.
Hold yourself ready to achieve your goals.
If you can prepare yourself for success, do so.
If your dream requires training or homework, do it.
Eliminate every barrier you can.
Give yourself every chance to get there
and chances are you will.

I dream of things that never were and say, 'Why not?'
Robert Fitzgerald Kennedy

Be happy ...

Push your luck

You've got to be in it to win it.
Give yourself the best chance you can.
Try your hand.
Be sensible but have a real go.
Pause and think:
if you don't try, will you regret it?
Go your hardest.

You miss one hundred per cent of the shots you don't take.

Wayne Gretzky

Be happy ...

Learn to swim

Swimming opens a world
of beauty and grace.
Water is essential to life.
It is your friend.
Allow yourself to meld with it.
Feel it support you.
Move like a dolphin.
Embrace the solitude.

Swim with the tide.

Anonymous

Be happy ...

Look for the inner beauty

We all have it.
Although some camouflage it very well.
And some hide it deep inside.
Take the time to search for it.
It's always there.
And the reward is worth the effort.

The most important things in life are not things.

Anonymous

Be happy ...

Stand on your own two feet

You can't find real fulfilment unless you do.
You can't flourish in someone else's shadow.
Take the risks.
Endure the falls.
Learn from them.
Enjoy the self-respect.
Savour the freedom.

The worst loneliness is not to be comfortable with yourself.

Mark Twain

Be happy ...

Put the past behind you

You can't change it,
so don't wear it like a chain.
Understand it.
Learn from it.
Turn the experience into a positive.
Use it to look ahead.

I will go anywhere provided it be forward.

Dr David Livingstone

Be happy ...

Find your artistic side

Every child has one.
As we grow up,
it may be denied,
or diminished,
or constrained,
or mocked.
But it's still there.
Look for it.
Discover it.
Release it.

One eye sees, the other feels.

Paul Klee

Be happy ...

Learn something every day

Every day, open your mind to something new.
It can come from nature, from others or from within.
Be aware.
Question the mundane.
Allow new things into your consciousness.
Relish the challenge.

Everybody is ignorant, only on different subjects.

Will Rogers

Be happy ...

Give credit

It brings reciprocal benefits to giver and receiver.
It liberates the giver
and renews the receiver's faith.
It transforms relationships
and forges trust.
It encourages greater effort.
It's the right thing to do.

Credit where credit is due.

Anonymous

Be happy ...

Amaze yourself

We use such a small amount of our capacity.
We constantly err on the side of caution.
Take the leap.
Extend yourself.
Move out of your comfort zone.
It's worth the risk.

Boldness has genius, power and magic in it.

Johann Wolfgang von Goethe

Be happy ...

Honour a veteran

We owe them so much.
Our freedom.
Our future.
They rarely ask for anything.
The least they deserve is recognition for their sacrifices.
A simple thank you will mean much to them.
Ask them about their personal stories
and you will be richly rewarded.

Old soldiers never die; they just fade away.

General Douglas MacArthur

Be happy ...

Do the right thing

It sounds so obvious.
Our inner compass is rarely wrong.
But we often ignore it
or avoid it.
Take notice of it.
Act on your feeling.
The satisfaction is well worth it.

Perfect kindness acts without thinking of kindness.

Lao-Tzu

Be happy ...

Rise to the occasion

Most of us live quietly on the fringes.
We're content to let others take centre stage.
Stay in the shadows or stride into the light.
You'll know when the time is right.
Take your chance.
Make it count.

When a decision has to be made, make it.
There is no totally right time for anything.

General George S. Patton

Be happy ...

Astral travel

We all need a change of scenery at some time.
When you can't make a physical change,
do it in your mind.
Let your imagination run free.
Fly at will.
Visit your dream locations.
Explore your dream locations.
Explore the possibilities.

The real voyage of discovery consists not in seeking new landscapes
but in having new eyes.

Marcel Proust

Be happy ...

Avert a disaster

If you foresee a problem,
however big or small,
you must act.
Think through the consequences.
Consider the damage.
Find the courage to speak up.

Courage is only the accumulation of small steps.

George Konrad

Be happy ...

Develop a backbone

If you've endured oppression,
if you've bowed to pressure,
if you've failed to fight back,
stop being the doormat.
Look within.
Respect yourself.
Decide what's really important to you.
Draw your boundaries.
Fight for them.

You must do the thing you think you can't do.

Eleanor Roosevelt

Be happy ...

Bare your soul

It can be wonderfully liberating,
but it's a gift to bestow with discernment.
The time and place must be right,
and, even more importantly, so must the person.
It takes courage to be vulnerable.
Feel the freedom.

The less you open your heart to others, the more your heart suffers.

Deepak Chopra

Be happy ...

Bite your tongue

When your blood is boiling,
and every instinct is telling you to shout back,
hold your tongue.
It can prevent damage to others
or save you regrets.
It can even give you an advantage,
as you maintain control.

If you are patient in one moment of anger,
you will avoid one hundred days of sorrow.

Chinese proverb

Be happy ...

Blaze a trail

Many of us fear change,
but it can often liberate and revitalise.
It doesn't have to be big.
Take a different route to work.
Try a new dish.
Learn a new language.
Breaking new grounds brings great satisfaction.

Begin difficult things while they are easy.

Lao-Tzu

Be happy ...

Break the cycle

When you're in a rut,
first, recognise the cycle in which you're trapped.
Then consider ways to break out of it.
Most of our restrictions are imaginary.
Many disappear simply by viewing things differently.
Others need a different plan,
but when you put your mind to it,
there's always a plan.

The attempt and not the deed confounds us.

William Shakespeare

Be happy ...

Care

Too often we rush through life
and people and things seem like props in a movie.
Take the time to look about you.
The important things will stand out.
These are the things to care about.

Is not love, even as time is, undivided and paceless?

Kahlil Gibran

Be happy ...

Celebrate

Life is too short not to celebrate.
Too often we concentrate on our failures,
or the negatives we encounter.
Enjoy the successes.
Savour the victories, big or small.
Make them memorable and worthwhile
and you're more likely to repeat them.

Laughter is wine for the soul.

Sean O'Casey

Be happy ...

Channel your energies

Sometimes we have to be single-minded.
It's the only way to achieve some goals.
We have to draw on
all our energy,
all our skills,
all our determination.
When we do, there's very little we can't accomplish.

Concentration comes out of a combination of confidence and hunger.
Arnold Palmer

Be happy ...

Clear the air

The longer we let problems fester,
the more damage they cause.
Confronting them always seems far worse
than it turns out to be.
Once you take the first step, most problems evaporate.
Deal with things.
Then you can get on with the journey
and leave the baggage behind.

If you know the enemy and you know yourself,
you need not fear the result of a hundred battles.

Sun Tzu

Be happy ...

Reach closure

Without closure,
wounds remain open,
hurt continues,
fear lingers.
Only by facing the fear,
righting the wrong,
saying farewell,
can we achieve peace of mind
and move forward.

Forgiveness does not change the past, but it does enlarge the future.
Paul Boese

Be happy ...

Confront your fears

So easy to say.
So difficult to do.
But until you face your fears,
you're always looking back.
You're a diminished version of yourself.
Do it by degrees,
do it with the help of others,
but stare down your fears.
Watch yourself grow as the fears shrink.

I'm never afraid of what I know.

Anna Sewell

Be happy ...

Cut your losses

Every good poker player knows it:
sometimes you have to throw in your hand.
The trick is knowing when to fight on
and when to bail out.
A good general rule:
when it's causing more harm than good,
it's time to leave it.

Being able to persist is not the most important thing—
the ability to start over is.

F. Scott Fitzgerald

Be happy ...

Have a massage

Never underestimate the power of touch.
It reassures and soothes,
relaxes and revitalises.
In expert hands, it nourishes and restores body and spirit.
It brings great satisfaction to giver and receiver.

They reached out their hands in longing for the further shore.

Virgil

Be happy ...

Delegate

It's one of the most valuable
—and most underused—skills.
It's not about avoiding responsibility.
It's a positive action.
Give someone the chance to be part of the team.
Allow the receiver to show initiative
and the giver to grow.

A leader is a man who can adapt principles to circumstances.
General George S. Patton

Be happy ...

Deliver

So often we bail out before finishing a task.
We'll always find excuses to justify it,
but then we live in the shadow of unfulfilled promises.
Whenever you can, move out of these shadows.
No matter how long it takes,
whether big or small,
finish the job.
You'll be amazed at the freedom it brings.

Give us the tools and we will finish the job.

Sir Winston Churchill

Be happy ...

Do your own thing

Everywhere, we're urged to conform.
To join the club.
To be like everyone else.
Resist the urge.
Look inside and discover the essential you.
Be true to yourself.
Follow your own path.

Don't compromise yourself. You're all you've got.

Janis Joplin

Be happy ...

Emerge from the shadows

You don't have to grab the limelight,
but don't live in the shadows of others.
Claim your place under the sun.
You can do it on your own terms.
You don't have to push others aside.
For your dignity and self-esteem, stand your ground.
Watch others' opinions of you rise.

Whether you think you will succeed or not—you're right.

Henry Ford

Be happy ...

Lose the stress

It's holding you back.
It's stifling your creativity.
It may even be killing you.
Locate the stresses in your life.
Isolate them.
Challenge them.
Replace them with alternatives:
change, meditation, exercise.

A field that has rested gives a beautiful crop.

Ovid

Be happy ...

Downshift

Discard some of that landfill we all accumulate.
Pare back unnecessary material baggage.
You'll discard a lot of mental and spiritual baggage as well.
It will open real meaning in your life.
You'll view things with renewed clarity.
You'll step off on new paths.

Think simple. Reduce the whole of its parts into the simplest terms,
getting back to first principles.

Frank Lloyd Wright

Be happy ...

Make the call yourself

Too often we allow others to choose our path.
That's usually the line of least resistance.
It provides a built-in excuse should things go awry,
but it also brings the least satisfaction.
Take the responsibility.
Shoulder the risks.
Explore the possibilities.
Make the call.
Enjoy the rewards.

A man who makes no mistakes does not usually make anything.
Edward John Phelps

Be happy ...

Take control of your health

You're only granted one body.
Think about how you treat it.
Most of us take better care of our cars.
Take a positive, proactive view.
Learn about your health needs.
Give your body the food, the exercise
and the rest it deserves.
It will repay you and those who love you.

If anything is sacred, the human body is sacred.

Walt Whitman

Be happy ...

Clean Up

No matter how long the mess has been there,
no matter how powerful the urge is to leave it there,
make the effort to clean it up.
It's worth it.
It opens up new horizons.
It brings freshness.
It opens up new perspectives.

Our life is frittered away with detail ... simplify, simplify.
Henry David Thoreau

Be happy ...

Say no

No sounds so simple,
but many people find it almost impossible to say.
They lack confidence.
They fear giving offence.
But when you know it's right—
when you know you'll regret it if you don't say it—
have courage.
Say no.
Other options will arise.
Others will respect you.

Which part of 'no' don't you understand?

Anonymous

Be happy ...

Prioritise

It's worth the time and the effort.
Consider the options before you.
Mull over the relative importance
of your tasks and duties.
Assign weight to each one.
Attack them in order of importance.
You'll be stunned at how that will free you up.
And how many seemingly pressing things
fade into insignificance.

A pint of sweat will save a gallon of blood.

General George S. Patton

Be happy ...

Slow down

We miss so much as we rush headlong through life.
Take the time to observe.
Allow yourself to weigh options.
Listen to alternatives.
Deliberate over decisions.
Focus your energy on one thing at a time.
Widen your vision.

Everything that happens to you is your teacher. The secret is to sit at
the feet of your own life and be taught by it.

Mahatma Gandhi

Be happy ...

Have a luxurious bath

When the stress is getting to you,
when you're tied up in knots,
take time out.
Fill a warm bath.
Throw in the bath salts.
Close the door.
Turn out the lights.
Go on a mini retreat.
Embrace the silence, the solitude
and the gentle warmth.
Emerge with your batteries recharged.

Too much of a good thing is wonderful.

Armistead Maupin

Be happy ...

Look up an old friend

It can be a sobering reality check
or a warm journey back in time.
Either way it is a journey worth taking.
Old friends act as measuring sticks.
They strip away the trimmings and heavy layers of your life.
They are mirrors to your soul.

A friend is a present you give yourself.

Robert Louis Stevenson

Be happy ...

Trace your family tree

It's a fascinating exercise.
It gives a feeling of continuity.
It answers many questions
and poses many more.
Show your heritage.
Reveal your tribe.
Draw the world closer together.

If the past cannot teach the present and the father cannot teach the son,
then history need not have bothered to go on and the world has wasted a
great deal of time.

Russell Hoban

Be happy ...

Master a new craft

Open yourself to new horizons.
Explore the potential of your skills
and your artistic abilities.
Find the right challenge.
It will bring satisfaction and joy.

We must use time as a tool not as a couch.

John Fitzgerald Kennedy

Be happy ...

Focus

It's so easy to dissipate our energies,
to dilute our creativity on too many tasks at once.
Virtuosos apply all their skill and energy
to one aim at a time.
Select your key tasks.
Concentrate on one at a time.
Avoid distractions.
Marshall your skills.
Direct all your energies at your target.

Things which matter most must never be at the mercy of things that
matter least.

Johann Wolfgang von Goethe

Be happy ...

Greet the sun

Rise before dawn.
Find a vantage point with a wide vista.
Wait for the first warming rays.
Feel their strength, their vitality.
Observe the world as it wakes around you.
Feel the renewal.

One touch of nature makes the whole world kin.

William Shakespeare

Be happy ...

Give something back

Most of us spend a lot of time taking.
Whenever you can, take time to give back.
Whether it's love or knowledge, power or money,
take the opportunity.
It allows you to grow.
It enriches the lives of others.
The rewards are often intangible, but they are great.

The quality of mercy is not strained ... it is twice blessed:
it blesseth him that gives and him that takes.

William Shakespeare

Be happy ...

Start a diary

Make your personal record,
your unique view of the world.
Keep it secure.
Write from your heart,
with passion,
without fear.
A diary brings perspective.
It diminishes anger.
It allows reflection.

The mind is its own place. In itself it can make a heaven or hell,
and a hell out of heaven.

John Milton

Be happy ...

Get political

When your passions are storming,
when your inner beliefs are aggrieved,
when you can no longer sit passively and watch,
take a stand.
Get logical and try to make changes.
Figure out the politics and the power balances.
Then act with decisiveness and persistence.

The one thing that doesn't bide by majority rule is a person's conscience.
Harper Lee

Be happy ...

Think global

Many of our problems start locally but spread globally.
If you believe strongly enough,
you can make a difference.
Widen your vision.
With today's communications, the world is a village.
Start small: one on one.
Then with passion and purpose, spread your word.
There are no boundaries.

Your playing small doesn't serve the world.

Marianne Williamson

Be happy ...

Start a new career

Allow yourself to constantly evolve.
Consider alternatives without bias.
Encourage your skills.
Be open to the new.
Welcome the challenges.
Find mentors.
Take the plunge.

I'm neither an optimist nor a pessimist, but a possibilist.

Max Lerner

Be happy ...

Find freedom

Too often we make our own cages:
of the mind
or the heart.
We have the keys to unlock them.
We only need the will to use them.
Unlock your heart, love freely.
Unlock your mind, live freely.

Your freedom and mind cannot be separated.

Nelson Mandela

Be happy ...

Unleash your imagination

Our minds' powers are virtually unlimited
and largely untapped.
With imagination we can create new worlds
and improve old ones.
Live our wildest dreams
and dream our wildest lives.
Imagination has neither rules nor boundaries.

Dreams are the language of creation.

Bernie Siegel

Be happy ...

Manage your time

It's one of our most precious assets,
and we don't know how much of it we have.
Value it highly.
Devote it to the most important things:
your family,
your loved ones,
your friends.
Then apportion it to your career.
Not the other way round.

The best and most beautiful things in the world cannot be seen
or even touched, they must be felt with the heart.

Helen Keller

Be happy ...

Ask 'what if?'

Too often we simply accept things the way they are.
Why not look at the things that aren't there
and ask why?
Consider the alternatives.
Look for other options.
Go back to first principles.
Forge new paths.
Dream boldly.

If you always do what you've always done,
you'll always get what you've always got.

Anonymous

Be happy ...

Find a soulmate

To have a soulmate, you must be one.
It's usually a natural selection:
soulmates find each other.
But you must be receptive.
It's a beautiful, rewarding friendship,
with a strong spiritual element.
It can't be manufactured or forced.
To find yours you must look outwards, not inwards.

A single soul dwelling in two bodies.

Aristotle

Be happy ...

Ask for directions

We all need help sometimes.
Asking someone for help honours them.
It may require a dose of humility,
but it's worth it.
It saves time.
It revitalises your quest.
It adds new dimensions.

Rather light a candle than complain about darkness.

Chinese proverb

Be happy ...

Cherish your friends

You can count your true friends on one hand.
They provide some of our best memories.
The real joy of friendship is when you give.
To make a friend, give someone your friendship.
They will reciprocate.
Treasure your friends.

A friend is a person with whom I may be sincere.
Before him I may think aloud.

Ralph Waldo Emerson

Be happy ...

Reassess your work

Your career is not you.
It's not your life, it's your job.
You can always expand your horizons
or change direction.
If you decide to change, remain positive.
Find a new work challenge that inspires you.
Explore it.
Then chase it with passion.

Victory belongs to the most persevering.

Napoleon Bonaparte

Be happy ...

Forgive

Forgiving releases us.
Until we do it we're imprisoned.
It allows us to draw a line and look ahead.
It empowers us.
It gives us positive energy.
It opens up the future.

Good, to forgive: best, to forget.

Robert Browning

Be happy ...

Hear both sides

How often do we make snap judgements.
Usually, they're based on second-hand facts.
Take the trouble to explore both sides.
Find the primary sources.
Ask the simple questions.
Compare the answers.
Only then form your views.

We don't see things the way they are, we see them as we are.

Anaïs Nin

Be happy ...

Seek authenticity

Seek out the things that really matter.
Peer through the fog of advertising and fads.
Value the genuine
in people and in objects.
Allow your heart to take a role.

Not everything that can be counted counts,
and not everything that counts can be counted.

Albert Einstein

Be happy ...

Find the humour

It's there in everything we do.
It shortens hours,
eases pain,
spreads joy.
It builds teamwork and makes work lighter.
It makes you welcome.

Good humour is one of the best articles of dress one can wear in society.
William Makepeace Thackeray

Be happy ...

Tell the truth

The truth always fights to break out
and it usually succeeds.
Lies are a burden.
They entangle us and weigh us down.
It's not worth the struggle.
Telling the truth clears the air.
It liberates.

It is an immense ocean that surrounds the island of truth.

Francis Bacon

Be happy ...

Ask the tough questions

Ask them of yourself.
There are so many:
Who are you?
Why are you here?
Where are you going?
How can you be the best you can?
Answering them is the real adventure.

If we knew what it was we were doing, it would not be called research,
would it?

Albert Einstein

Be happy ...

Say a kind word

A simple word of praise can lift a heavy heart.
It makes the giver a better person
and gives the receiver hope and faith.
It's usually reciprocated.
It gives life greater purpose.

Kind words can be short and easy to speak ...
but their echoes are truly endless.

Mother Teresa

Be happy ...

Enjoy a sunset

No artist can truly capture its aura.
No film can reproduce its splendour.
Watch it alone or with a loved one.
Drink it in.
Feel humble but feel alive.
Be inspired by its magnificence.

Everything has its beauty but not everyone sees it.

Confucius

Be happy ...

Make a difference

Individuals can make a difference.
You can too.
When you see the chance, make the effort.
Just trying will bring you satisfaction and honour.

Do more than is required of you.

General George S. Patton

Be happy ...

Have faith

In a cynical world, faith is all the more important.
Nurture your faith
in yourself,
in your beliefs,
in love,
in kindness.
Recognise its mystical power.
Embrace it.
Use its strength.

Faith sees the invisible, feels the intangible and achieves the impossible.
Anonymous

Be happy ...

Assert yourself

Stepping out of your comfort zone offers so much.
It changes the way you look at yourself.
It changes the way others view you.
It alters the dynamics of relationships.
It opens new paths for you.

Wheresoever you go, go with all your heart.

Confucius

Be happy ...

Try

Whatever you do,
however hard the challenge,
always look for the light.
Use all your strengths.
Draw on your reserves.
Never concede.
Have a go.

Real education is bringing the best out of yourself.

Mohandas K. Gandhi

Be happy ...

Accept only the best

Appreciate great achievements.
Consider the skills, energy and dedication they demand.
Imagine the satisfaction.
Reset some of your own goals.
Lift your sights and your benchmarks.
Avoid mediocrity.
Strive for greatness.

Your own resolution to success is more important than
any other one thing.

Abraham Lincoln

Be happy ...

Keep abreast of the news

News is an ongoing lesson in living,
a constant source of wonderment.
It explains the past.
It unravels the present.
It arms you for the future.

It's your world. You're a shareholder, take an active interest in it.

Anonymous

Be happy ...

Watch a spider at work

Notice the endless patience.
Appreciate the determination.
See the innate beauty of the designs.
Observe the drama.
Learn the lessons.

Whatever is flexible and loving will tend to grow.
Whatever is rigid and blocked will wither and die.

Lao-Tzu

Be happy ...

Arrest the slide

It takes real character.
Sometimes it demands courage.
It means accepting responsibility
and avoiding the lines of least resistance.
When you can do something to change things, do it.
Acting will bring lasting satisfaction
and open great possibilities.

You must be the change you want to see in the world.

Mohandas K. Gandhi

Be happy ...

Find perspective

As the world rushes by,
take time to pause.
Look out from within.
Observe like a camera:
without judgement,
without rancour.
Recognise the authentic, important things.
Give them priority.

And in the end it's not the years in your life that count,
it's the life in your years.

Abraham Lincoln

Be happy ...

Be the best you can

This can transform your life.
When you commit to your personal quest,
unimagined possibilities open to you.
Consider how you'd like to be remembered.
Then strive to match your potential.
Here lies your real value,
and the path will reveal itself.

We must understand what we have been, to decide what we will become.
John Faulkner

Be happy ...

Be yourself

It sounds simple but it requires great faith.
Despite the doubters, the detractors,
the risks of failure and the self-doubt,
dare to believe in yourself.
If you're not prepared to back yourself,
don't expect others to.
If you have confidence in yourself,
so will others.

He can, who believes he can.

Proverb

Be happy ...

Be kind

As we rush through life,
we miss many of its greatest rewards.
Take the gentler road.
Take time to talk to people.
Learn about their lives
and their loved ones.
It will broaden your life and give you compassion.
Accept their kindnesses.
Be kind in return.

Kindness is more important than wisdom, and the recognition of this
is the beginning of wisdom.

Theodore Isaac Rubin

Be happy ...

Right a wrong

It's centred deep in us.
We all know the right thing to do.
Avoiding it gnaws at our heart of hearts.
It tarnishes our spirit.
No matter how long it's been, repair the situation.
Do what is in your power to make it right.
It will free your spirit.

Prove all things; hold fast that which is good.

The Bible

Be happy ...

Attend to the little things

The small things in your life often have a deep impact.
It can be as trivial as trimming your nails.
A simple act of renewal:
a sign of optimism and care.
It raises self-esteem.
It promises better things.

The breath of life is in the sunlight and the hand of life is in the wind.
Kahlil Gibran

Be happy ...

Design your own future

Consider the possibilities in your life,
not what seem to be the realities.
Look at what you can do,
not what you are doing.
Realities are often just misconceptions.
Take a different view.
Find your opinions.
Create your own future.

You can analyse the past but you have to design the future.

Edward de Bono

Be happy ...

Find your inner leader

We each have the potential to lead.
To some it comes naturally.
To most it's cloaked in self-doubt and fear.
For some it means leading on a big stage.
For most it means taking a lead in the small things,
as a parent,
as a friend,
in a family,
at work.
The power is within you.

Who looks outside, dreams. Who looks inside, awakens.

Carl Jung

Be happy ...

Know yourself

We think we do.
We know things about ourselves nobody else does.
But are we honest with ourselves?
It comes with wisdom
and accepting our imperfections.
The more we know about ourselves,
the more freedom we have.

The spirit is the true self.

Cicero

Be happy …

Find your passions

Embrace the things in life you're passionate about.
You'll be transported.
Your path will be clearer.
Your tread will be more certain.
Feel the power.
Enjoy the journey.

Follow your bliss, and doors will open where there were no doors before.
Joseph Campbell

Be happy ...

See beauty

It's in everything.
Sometimes it's shining out at us,
sometimes it's hidden deep within.
Look for the deeper beauty
in nature's balances,
in the human spirit,
in beautiful friendships,
the beautiful mind,
the beautiful heart.

Beauty is eloquent even when silent.

Proverb

Be happy ...

Rewire yourself

Let your skills constantly grow.
Challenge them.
Build on them.
Share them.
And draw from others' skills.
Use your experience.
But keep it current.

They know enough who know how to learn.

Henry Adams

Be happy ...

Lose the fear of failing

We can't make progress without failing.
Fear of failing holds us back.
Most successful people fail more often than they succeed,
but they persist.
Failing is just improving your chances
of succeeding next time.
Allow yourself the possibility of failing.

I would sooner fail than not be among the greatest.

John Keats

Be happy ...

Find dignity

Live with style.
Win, lose or draw with elegance.
Carry yourself lightly.
Give more than you take.
Praise more than you criticise.
Tread gently on the earth.

Better wit than wealth.

Proverb

Be happy ...

Move to the edge

We set our boundaries for safety,
or from fear, or because of habit.
Test them.
See why you drew them.
Push against them.
Break through them.
Find your edge.
Feel the exhilaration.

For what is freedom, but the unfettered use of all the powers which God
for use had given.

Samuel Taylor Coleridge

Be happy ...

Think

How often we don't.
Or we act, then we think.
Take the time.
Avoid distractions.
Concentrate.
Wash problems through your mind.
Consider consequences.
Find options.
Project ahead.

Thinking is seeing.

Honore de Balzac

Be happy ...

Do something great

Never underestimate your potential
or discount your ability.
Most great achievements are based on perseverance.
Believe in yourself.
Persist.
When others give in, keep going.
When you falter, have faith in yourself
and surge ahead.

Be not afraid of greatness.

William Shakespeare

Be happy ...

Hope

Hope is a central part of our life force.
Never surrender your hope.
We know life comes in cycles
and an upturn can be just around the corner.
Hope helps us struggle through the desperate times.
It guides us through the dark.
While you have options, you have hope.

Hope well and have well.

Proverb

Be happy ...

Make your own decisions

Take advice.
Seek information.
Draw on others' experience.
Confirm your views,
but make your own choices.
Set your own course.
Be responsible for your own life.

No decision is difficult to make if you will get all of the facts.
General George S. Patton

Be happy ...

Share wisdom

It's rewarding.
It brings benefits to both giver and receiver.
Pass on your hard-won experience,
especially where it can stop suffering or pain.
Hand on knowledge generously.
It will be repaid tenfold.

If you have, give. If you learn, teach.

Maya Angelou

Be happy ...

Find peace

Nobody can prevent you from finding peace.
Unless you empower them.
If something is stopping you from reaching it,
act on it.
If it's outside your powers,
stop worrying about it.
Peace comes from within.

A peace above earthly dignities. A still and quiet conscience.
William Shakespeare

Be happy ...

Rebound

Sometimes the down times seem endless,
but they're part of a cycle.
What goes around, comes around.
Keep the faith.
It may take time.
Wait for your time.
Bounce back.

The struggle is my life. I will continue fighting for freedom
until the end of my days.

Nelson Mandela

Be happy ...

Take your chance

You'll know when the time is right.
When you are the best equipped,
the most experienced or the most capable.
You owe it to yourself to grasp the chance.
Trust your instincts.
Show the way.

A leader is a man who can adapt principles to circumstances.
General George S. Patton

Be happy ...

Be young at heart

It doesn't mean fighting against time.
We must grow.
We can even age.
But we can stay young in heart and mind.
Look with young eyes.
Love with a young heart.
Recapture the wonderment.
Look forward with hope and optimism.

Youth has no age.

Pablo Picasso

Be happy ...

Remember

Our memories are a treasure trove,
our living photo album.
Take time to visit your memories.
Spool through them.
Enjoy them.
Learn from them.
Then add to them.

The richness of life lies in memories we have forgotten.

Cesare Pavese

Be happy ...

Be curious

Curiosity allows possibilities.
It keeps you fresh.
It acknowledges mysteries
and challenges them.
It's grounded in hope.
It validates our existence
and fans the inner fire.
To be curious is to be optimistic.

The most useful gift for a child at birth is curiosity.

Eleanor Roosevelt

Be happy ...

Listen to your body

Give it a chance to talk to you.
Learn the signs.
The feelings.
The messages.
Good and bad.
Heed its messages.
Respect your body.

Every man is the builder of a temple called his body.

Henry Thoreau

Be happy ...

Let go

Unload the things that weigh you down.
Lose the baggage:
regrets, grudges,
hatreds, jealousies, vendettas.
Feel yourself soar ahead.

We are what we repeatedly do.

Aristotle

Be happy ...

Start each day afresh

Every dawn brings unlimited possibilities.
It brings new challenges.
It opens new hope.
Don't be shackled by yesterday.
Look ahead with optimism.
Create your future afresh each day.

You cannot step twice into the same river.

Heraclitus

Be happy ...

Find compromise

Things are rarely black or white.
There are always other views
or other ways of achieving consensus.
Isolate what you hope to achieve.
The path to it may not be direct.
You may have to surrender ground to progress.
Keep your goal in mind.
Adapt your means to suit circumstances.

It doesn't matter whether it's a black cat or a white cat
as long as it catches the mouse.

Deng Xiao Ping

Be happy ...

Listen to children

The things they know are different
and fascinating.
You can learn from kids:
about them,
about you,
about life.
Remember your frustration
when you were a child
and people wouldn't listen to you.

It's all that the young can do for the old,
to shock them and keep them up to date.

George Bernard Shaw

Be happy ...

Accept change

Change is the only constant in life.
In nature, in society, in relationships, at work,
things change.
And they change constantly.
See it as part of the larger picture.
See it as normal.
Don't fight it.
Adapt to it.

They must often change who would be constant in
happiness and wisdom.

Confucius

Be happy ...

Persevere

Those who succeed are not necessarily the most gifted.
They are the ones who never give in.
Inspiration is just the start.
Perseverance is what brings things to fruition.
Whatever the obstacle,
whatever the opposition,
however long it takes,
see things through.

Patience and time do more than force and rage.

Jean de la Fontaine

Be happy ...

Learn from mistakes

Take a wider view.
Look at the patterns in your life.
If there are recurring problems,
maybe there are recurring mistakes.
Mistakes don't always look the same.
Find the pattern.
Change your behaviour.
Learn.

Experience is the mother of wisdom.

Proverb

Be happy ...

Discover your métier

Some know it from childhood.
Some never find it.
But we all have special talents.
Take the time to explore yours.
They may be disguised.
They may be undeveloped.
But trust your instincts.
Give yourself the opportunity.
They will be there.

Genius is merely a greater aptitude for patience.

Compte de Buffon

Be happy ...

Stop worrying

Separate the anxiety from the problem.
If you can't change things,
worrying about them won't help.
Allow things to take their course.
Options will open up.
Work out what you can do,
then do it.
When you stop worrying,
you think clearly.

Nothing in the affairs of men is worthy of great anxiety.

Plato

Be happy ...

Face your fears

Until you do, you remain in chains.
Never underestimate your courage.
Be positive. If necessary, take it in stages.
Often your fear is outdated,
or based on a misunderstanding or misapprehension.
Look it straight in the eye.
Once you break the spell, you're free.

They can conquer who believe they can.

John Dryden

Be happy ...

Befriend an animal

It expands your life
and widens your focus.
It makes you gentler,
more compassionate,
more tactile.
It brings great rewards:
unconditional love,
time for reflection
and warmth in your life.

To his dog every man is king.

Anonymous

Be happy ...

Learn to listen

Even when you have a point to make,
even when you're angry or frustrated,
pause and listen to the person talking to you.
Listen to the world around you.
Listen to your heart
and your loved ones.
Listen to their words.
Hear their unsaid messages.

Nothing is a waste of time if you use the experience wisely.

Auguste Rodin

Be happy ...

Laugh at yourself

It's easy to laugh at others,
much harder to laugh at ourselves.
But it's more rewarding.
It lightens our lives.
It brightens others' lives.
It builds self-confidence and self-worth.
It endears us to others.
And life is too short to take it too seriously.

Time spent laughing is time spent with the gods.

Japanese proverb

Be happy ...

Travel

Change the scenery of your life.
A chance to refresh,
to learn,
to compare,
to meet new people,
to make new friends,
to view things anew,
to grow.

When there is no fish in one spot, cast your net in another.

Chinese proverb

Be happy ...

Start again

Nothing stays the same.
Look at nature.
Use change wisely.
Like a sporting champion, change a losing game.
Keep things that matter.
Lose things that don't.
Set goals.
Start afresh.

Imagination is more important than knowledge.

Albert Einstein

Be happy ...

Be the best you can

How much of your potential have you reached?
Think about what has held you back.
For most of us it's fear:
fear of failure,
fear of the unknown,
sometimes even of success.
Confront that fear.
Your potential will open to you.

All that you achieve and all that you fail to achieve is the direct result of
your thoughts.

James Allen

Be happy ...

Widen your wisdom

Look beyond your normal limits.
Imagine the bigger picture.
Consider the next step,
the flow-on effect.
Opportunities will appear.
Motivations will become clear.
Perspectives will emerge.

One must live the way one thinks or end up thinking the way one has lived.
Paul Bourget

Be happy ...

Sleep on it

When problems are bearing down on you
and you're feeling overwhelmed,
take a break.
Put them to the back of your mind.
Go for a walk.
If you can't break the impasse, sleep on them.
You'll be amazed how many are resolved by morning.

It is a common experience that a problem, difficult at night, is resolved in
the morning after the committee of sleep has worked on it.

John Steinbeck

Be happy ...

Set new goals

All great athletes seek personal bests.
It's a wonderful approach to life.
Always seek new challenges,
especially those that stretch your capabilities.
But remember, it's not the goal that's important:
it's the quest that brings the benefits.

The journey, not the arrival, matters.

Paul Theroux

Be happy ...

Chill out

Take time out.
Walk in the park.
Browse in a bookstore.
Relax in a cafe.
Go for a run, or swim.
Have a laugh with friends.
Break the cycle.
Then return with your batteries recharged.

The hours that make us happy, make us wise.

John Mansfield

Be happy ...

Find your tribe

We all have a natural home:
in the country,
by the sea,
in the city.
It's in our blood.
Here we're most content.
Here we flourish.
Here lies peace.

Until you make peace with who you are, you'll never be content with
what you have.

Doris Mortman

Be happy ...

Learn tolerance

'Do unto others ...'
It's a sound approach to life.
If we took the time to put ourselves in others' shoes,
we'd do a lot of things differently.
Tolerance is often just being genuine in our actions.
It usually means 'walking our talk'.
It's almost always repaid in kind.

As you sow, so shall you reap.

The Bible

Be happy ...

Be flexible

Keep your mind open.
Don't rush to conclusions.
Be wary of unshakeable certainty.
Allow for unthought-of possibilities.
It will broaden your vision.
It will strengthen your final viewpoint.

Time cools, time clarifies; no mood can be maintained quite unaltered
through the course of hours.

Thomas Mann

Be happy ...

Check your bearings

Often we can only see where we're going
when we look at where we've been.
Take a long view.
Be sure you're on track
and that you're travelling with the right companions.
Then resume your journey with confidence.

Our conscience must catch up to our reason, otherwise we are lost.
Goran Carstedt

Be happy ...

Break new ground

Take the initiative.
Set the guidelines.
Winners have plans.
Losers have excuses.
If you wait for someone else to move,
you're playing by their rules.
The risks are higher,
but so are the rewards.

Taking the first step, uttering a new word is what people fear most.
Fyodor Dostoyevsky

Be happy ...

Find your poetry

Write from your heart.
Let the words flow.
Poems can heal.
They can transmit love.
They can release sorrow.
They can reveal dreams.
They are a beautiful gift.

The dream is an involuntary kind of poetry.

Jean Paul Richter

Be happy ...

Break your routine

Move out of your comfort zone.
The slightest change can empower.
It highlights the options.
It reveals new horizons.
It provides fresh views.
It invigorates.

Life is largely a matter of expectations.

Horace

Be happy ...

Embrace your creative side

Never underestimate your creative powers.
Give them full reign.
Allow them to flourish.
Explore the things that give you fulfilment:
art, music, crafts, writing, gardening.
Extend your creativity to your work.
It will give great satisfaction.
It will draw others to you.

Wisdom begins in wonder.

Sophocles

Be happy ...

Plan ahead

It brings hope.
It takes you out of the daily grind.
Small plans first,
with realistic goals,
build confidence,
then make bigger plans with bigger goals.
Always have plans.

You are young at any age if you're planning for tomorrow.

Anonymous

Be happy ...

Be a mentor

It's a two-way street.
You pass on your hard-won skills and wisdom,
you receive insight and friendship.
You're a conduit for knowledge.
You ease the path.
In return, you'll see life through different eyes
and you'll learn more than you teach.

Experience is what you get while you're looking for something else.
Federico Fellini

Be happy ...

Spend time with your parents

Don't leave it too late.
Remember how much they've given you.
Be grateful for their sacrifices.
Repay their love.
Enjoy their company.
Enhance their lives.

Opportunities do not wait.

Greek proverb

Be happy ...

Volunteer

It's part of our culture.
It's the spine of our communities.
It can be so rewarding.
It creates confidence.
It builds friendships.
It fulfils our spiritual needs.
It promotes natural leadership.

Leadership is creating a world to which other people want to belong.
Giles Pajou

Be happy ...

Live in the moment

Too often we worry about the future,
and brood about the past.
Focus your energy on the present.
In the present you're as alive as you can be.
Your decisions are spontaneous.
Your heart is open.
Your spirit is free.

Be happy while you're living, for you're a long time dead.

Scottish proverb

Be happy ...

Think laterally

Employ both sides of your brain.
Connect your imagination to your reasoning.
Gather information, use your intelligence.
Then consider things creatively.
Break away from analysis and judgement.
Move into your dreamworld.

Nothing happens unless first a dream.

Carl Sandburg

Be happy ...

Spread love

It binds us together.
It validates our lives.
It gives us meaning.
It brings compassion.
It lets us see with new eyes.

To love someone deeply gives you strength; being loved by someone
deeply gives you courage.

Lao-Tzu